HAL•LEONARD
INSTRUMENTAL
PLAY-ALONG

AUDIO
ACCESS
INCLUDED

PLAYBACK+
Speed • Pitch • Balance • Loop

CLARINET

PEACEFUL HYMNS

Audio arrangements by Peter Deneff

To access audio visit:
www.halleonard.com/mylibrary

Enter Code
4297-8755-9705-7356

T0057211

ISBN 978-1-70513-790-1

Visit Hal Leonard Online at
www.halleonard.com

Contact us:
Hal Leonard
7777 West Bluemound Road
Milwaukee, WI 53213
Email: info@halleonard.com

In Europe, contact:
Hal Leonard Europe Limited
42 Wigmore Street
Marylebone, London, W1U 2RN
Email: info@halleonardeurope.com

In Australia, contact:
Hal Leonard Australia Pty. Ltd.
4 Lentara Court
Cheltenham, Victoria, 3192 Australia
Email: info@halleonard.com.au

ABIDE WITH ME

CLARINET

Music by WILLIAM H. MONK

ALL CREATURES OF OUR GOD AND KING

CLARINET

Music from *Geistliche Kirchengesang*

ALL HAIL THE POWER OF JESUS' NAME

CLARINET

Music by OLIVER HOLDEN

ALL THROUGH THE NIGHT

CLARINET

Welsh Folksong

AMAZING GRACE

CLARINET

Traditional American Melody

BE THOU MY VISION

CLARINET

Traditional Irish

BLESSED ASSURANCE

CLARINET

Music by PHOEBE PALMER KNAPP

COME, THOU FOUNT OF EVERY BLESSING

CLARINET

Music from John Wyeth's *Repository of Sacred Music*

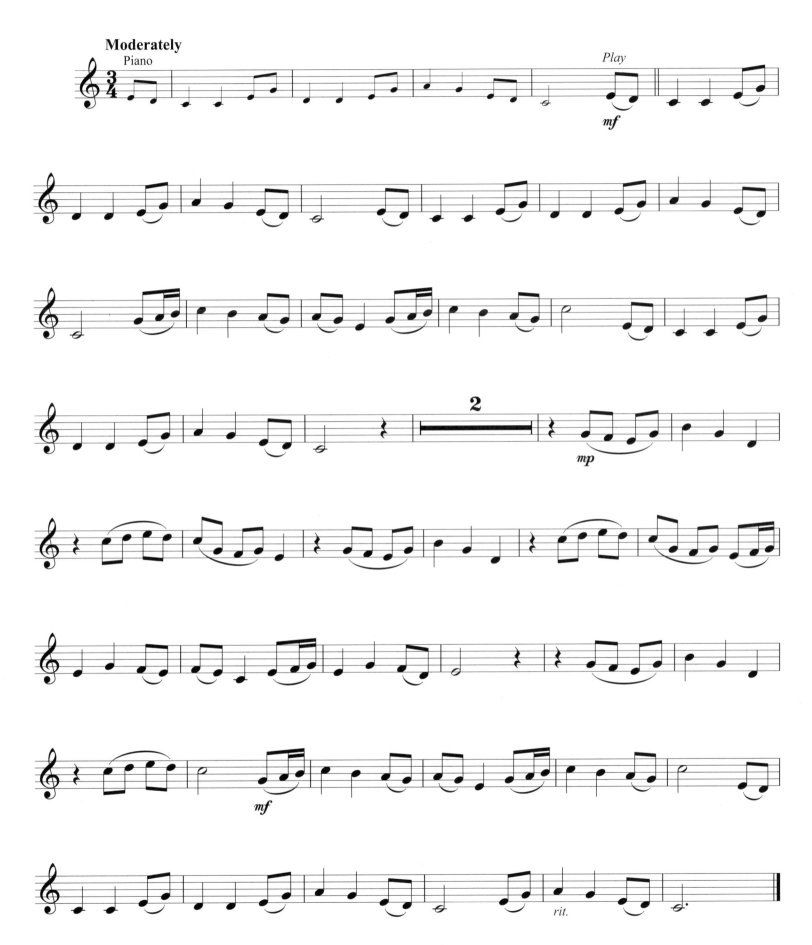

FAIREST LORD JESUS

CLARINET

Music from *Schlesische Volkslieder*

FOR THE BEAUTY OF THE EARTH

CLARINET

Music by CONRAD KOCHER

GREAT IS THY FAITHFULNESS

CLARINET

Music by WILLIAM M. RUNYAN

HOLY, HOLY, HOLY

CLARINET

Music by JOHN B. DYKES

HOW FIRM A FOUNDATION

CLARINET

Traditional music compiled by JOSEPH FUNK

I NEED THEE EVERY HOUR

CLARINET

Music by ROBERT LOWRY

IT IS WELL WITH MY SOUL

CLARINET

Music by PHILIP P. BLISS

JUST AS I AM

CLARINET

Music by WILLIAM B. BRADBURY

THE KING OF LOVE MY SHEPHERD IS

CLARINET

Traditional Irish Melody

LET ALL MORTAL FLESH KEEP SILENCE

CLARINET

17th Century French Carol

MY FAITH LOOKS UP TO THEE

CLARINET

Music by LOWELL MASON

NEARER, MY GOD, TO THEE

CLARINET

Music by LOWELL MASON

WERE YOU THERE WHEN THEY CRUCIFIED MY LORD?

CLARINET

Traditional

WHAT A FRIEND WE HAVE IN JESUS

CLARINET

Music by CHARLES C. CONVERSE

WONDROUS LOVE

CLARINET

Southern American Folk Hymn